CLEAVEMARK

Cleavemark

Stephanie Ellis Schlaifer

Printed in the United States of America
Book layout and cover design: Laura Theobald
Cover Image: Susanne N. Schlaifer
BOAAT Press is a publisher and builder of books.
ISBN 978-0-692-51027-8

BOAAT Press
6 Oklahoma Drive
Jackson, NJ 08527
www.boaatpress.com

for my mother
and her mother

Acknowledgments

Tremendous gratitude goes to the editors of the following magazines, in which these poems first appeared:

1913: A Journal of Forms
    "Cataract"

Carolina Quarterly
    "Native Plants and Animals"

Chicago Review
    "If she is a wall   we build"
    "Elevation: East"
    "Elevation: North"

Cimarron Review
    "Rolling Living Room"

Colorado Review
    "—not growing"
    "The tiles are pink   the tiles are black"

Delmar
    "Childproofing" (reprinted by Augury Books, fall 2013)
    "Susanne Cawood"
    "Tender" (reprinted in *SpringGun*, fall 2012)

elevenbulls
    "Pictures of the House Under Construction"

Fence
    "Everything you want to know about dishes"

Kestrel
    "Cleavemark Dr."
    "When the eye saw   it appeared"

Midway Journal
    "Upwards"

Observable Books
    "Elevation: West"

Sugar House Review
    "Similitude"

I would like to thank everyone at BOAAT, particularly Shane McCrae, for selecting this manuscript.

To my parents, for never saying "no" to a book, and not always saying "yes" to what I wrote.

To my sister, for showing me what magic is.

To my teachers and professors, writing and otherwise, for holding my feet to the fire (and, occasionally, bending the rules): Greg Hyde, Virginia Carnes, Jennifer Atkinson, Erin Belieu, James Galvin, Claudia Rankine, Cole Swensen, Ron Leax, Douglas Dowd, and especially Jeff Hamilton, for his bountiful insight and friendship.

To my writing group, particularly Lisa Pepper, for giving me endless inspiration and, sometimes, a good kick in the pants.

Thanks to all of the creative people in my life, who make everything unbelievably strange and wonderful, particularly Jeff Pike, Ben Kiel, Lisa Bulawsky, Jen Meyer, Augusta Ridley, Cheryl Wassenaar, and Jana Harper.

To my oldest, dearest friends—Margaret, Suzanne, Elizabeth, and Natalie, especially, for holding me together.

To Jessica Baran, Vieve Kaplan, Sarah Courteau, and Kerry Reilly, whose writing and company I could never possibly have enough of.

To Keith Wilhite, for all those Thursday nights writing at the Sanctuary.

And, above all, to my husband, Arny. I endeavor to deserve you.

A note on the text:
Some of the text is informed by or borrows from passages from the Old Testament, particularly the books of Psalms, Isaiah, and Job. I am eternally grateful to the staff at the Sanctuary in Iowa City, who thought to fish that old Bible out of the dumpster, thinking someone at the bar might need it someday. I did.

Contents

IN A DREAM
YOU SAW A WAY
TO SURVIVE
AND YOU WERE
FULL OF JOY

Jenny Holzer

———————————

FROM THE ENDS OF THE EARTH
I CALL TO YOU,
I CALL AS MY HEART GROWS FAINT;
LEAD ME TO THE ROCK
THAT IS HIGHER THAN I.

—Psalms, 61:2

Everything you want to know about Dishes

happens in a nest   stackable as
aloe   with a little teeth

                    it is the first wall hinging
all the house in happiness and death

                    the house is not so wide

the busy wall is the busy wall
and they are kept here

                    a throat's extent
                         in railing

the house is thin
as pivots:

                    living
living rounds the stair

the house is not so wide:
there is a door and a door

THE TILES ARE PINK   THE TILES ARE BLACK

the tiles are rosy   and often there were roses in the nest

the rosed commode—the fuzzy seat—

                                    the toilet rug that slenders

closers to your closets   extends itself
                a ramekin   a breadth

burnt fish
                    a parlor-herd

of slurry   I would rather be a clothespin
a scent that hunts itself to death

how weighty I am   still with you

            why do you keep your hand

in stock   in cups   in tempo of
the porcelain   a tender hole
of slip

            why do you keep it with you
the scent is bitter   purser on   said doorkeepers
said soap
                    do not touch the spigot metal
                    do not touch its mouth

                              —days and won't you
get in—
                    take a bath—

            the water to the cleanness of my hands

indelicate in calcium
                                        make

                    bubbles   place
            your lips:

            wet wood   Nanny   thread-bare

spool

            exfoliant/astringent

                        /you
                                    —get in
and with the soda
            she can clean the shower and her teeth
do not remove the ancient landmarks
            do not wear yourself   in dusting
                    why should your bed be taken

hand from under
            try to count them
            sand as sand
the light when it is gone

— NOT GROWING

it is dark.
                        the time
                                so getting

you cannot get in under

no dogs— the train yet—   not even weather

there is a reason to
            early early

if you need a reason to get up in the dark

The house is split around its oven—
            a cake there, rising,
                minutes in

no God yet
on the television—bands of color

            all the trees go
                    :sharpening

for things on earth are small

            iron sharpens iron

a door turns on its hinges,
swaying

—she gets up in it
the hour you have clocks for

Susanne Cawood

She was, before
Roger, Susanne
Nance; Sue, to her
brothers; Sue, with
the beautiful
legs and the bad
teeth, smirking to
hide them; smiling

through all that suit-
able, late-fifties
lavender, for
her mother; her
matching pillbox
hat and hatpins
in the pocket, in
the front, sticking

her. *Smile.* Stuck
in the drawer, with
the wrought iron
handle, are the
scissors—She used
to cut my hair
with those things, if
you can believe it:
Just a little
more over here...
God, it was so
uneven...and
those curls! —Toni
made a little
Tonette for little
girls who needed

curls for picture-
day; a bathroom,
Do-It-Yourself
home permanent,
complete with pink
rods and papers,
but not the iron
to flatten out

mistakes—Susanne
C, looking like a
little Sylvia,
wigged blonde, floating
a dark iris
in her eye, a
black shoe memory
stepping up a

stool, looking for
whatever makes
that milk taste so
good. She is not
supposed to have
it, but she's up
with her hands in
the cabinets,

reaching around
the cardamom,
the curry, the
pickling jar of
old pimentos
on the spare house
key, to find the
blown glass brown of

straight bourbon
vanilla, glowing
behind distilled
white vinegar.
One hand frees to
twist its lid
open before
she calls you, *Su—!!!*

God, it tasted
terrible.

Tender

For SRWS

You can see it from the boat—

that it's not the ocean;
that it is a lake.

The lake alone does not allow it—
the gull caught stale
in sail and rigging; feathers stick the anchor
bend, the anchor fluke—
the anchor's digging end.

The papers cannot say, of course:

he is not
survived;
Teddy Hays is dead.

The boats the lake ensures you see:
Sassy, Fool's Gold, Last Man Standing;

no Princess slips, but Lady D—
Ladies I and II.
I board the revised version, the second wife.
A rented yacht, upholstered in the 80s;
has berbered walls—
peach-pink,
gray-green,
the color taupe is.

* * *

You can see the shoreline
from the deck—an ice cream vendor's
selling bottled water. Two girls
empty one into the lake
and stuff it full of
limes and rum and sugar
(mindful of their dresses):
so much for a little Judith Leiber.

Inside I hear they serve champagne.
Champagne—why not,
it is a wedding.

      *　*　*

Helen's husband bought a boat.

She said
        —for fishing,
        for when he comes home on the weekends.

He asked her once

        A baby or a boat?
        Boat—
he said
        for fishing on the weekends.

She said she said
        I get to name it.

        What?
He said, when they went fishing.

        The Rough Draft—

She said, standing at the stern,

        —I'm pregnant.

If he were not himself, he would be a fisherman.

*   *   *

The deck shows where the sound comes from:
a Hasselblad of capping water,
the pilings water
beats and pins;
the netting mossed
and hairy as a lung,
the logs all stemming
starboard at the throat—Champagne!—
the Lady cramps
and nettles;
someone mends
a break, new paint—
Champagne! —here's to the sailors on the Dark Horse
(To Ted) here's to your classic schooner!
The working rig.
The boat's boat.

*   *   *

What to write,
the papers wrote.

We were told there would be fireworks.

Fireworks every Saturday shoot off Navy Pier.

After all, this is a wedding—so far they have only handed out kazoos.

I know, you were only hired for the night,
but my date would like to know where you keep the lifejackets,
and we would like to try them on.

What people own the Last Man Standing?

Yes.

I see.

And Sassy?

Yes, I know you were—

I cannot ask the sailors on the Dark Horse.

What sort of people name these boats?

You have to be the one to tell us.
Why it doesn't— didn't— won't you

Yes, I see—   Ted hanged himself, I know.

A plastic bag, rappelling line.

I know.   You were only hired for the night.

*   *   *

The papers wrote.

The ground is hard.
Too, it kills you.

The water stops
and it is cold
for digging.

Hot for Tennessee in April.
Even that far south.

Flat drafts come in through his fireplace.
Nuclear. No smoke.

      No, he didn't—
             left his things out

Had his things out
        —this is me—

articles, how-to's, CDs.

      No he didn't leave a—

*   *   *

Something like this came for Helen.
It got her rag rug easily;
the tabletop, the sofa's feet;
puzzles and the tops of frames;
nothing from the walls could stay.
Nothing wasn't clean.

The shape and size of her,
her shoes—the likeness of
a woman, resting.

Everything at rest is glass
or iron; fists and matches.
ropes and ropes.

ELEVATION: WEST

They have lids for this
They have soap for this
They have casseroles
and meals from meals
They have a chicken-in-the-pot   and

you must not wake the house

Near the stovetop   called the rangetop
there is a tin   there is a barrel
On top of the refrigerator/freezer
there is a canister of low-sodium potato chips
—a cookie jar that trains you
not to eat cookies

Fully-fitted   vented   steamed
the body can make sense of pain

        You can make that—

catchall   a cabinet

        There is salt

There is a container about the size of me

Childproofing

i.

My mother is reading a book
entitled *The Fearful Child,*
and in between pages 57 & 58,
there is a tiny yellow sticky labeled STEPHANIE.

I am the section of the chapter subtitled
"Overactive Imagination, Underactive Reasoning."

Apparently,
I am abnormal.
I have been
found out.

It is disappointing
to find that
I have not been mentioned in the forward.

Just the same,
my mother has penned me in.

The book was neatly blanketed
by *A Special Issue*
of *Martha Stewart Living*
lying underneath the nightstand
near the Better Homes and Gardens
Family Medical Guide.

One morning I found a kitchen knife
wedged between
the mattress and the box spring.

It is easier to be anthologized
than really in the dark.

I can make a doily from a tourniquet
from the queen Charisma sheets.

Somewhere there is an artist
commissioned to illustrate an erection,

trench mouth and nasturtium;
harelips, epileptic,
Convallaria majalis,
pinworms and

an itchy anus,
common,
accidental death;

I like to read
what my mother is reading:
fragrant, wide flowers.

ii.

Occasionally, we have company
over. They ask, "Why
do you have babies
in the basement?

It is odd—
they scratch so at the door."

My mother kept us there
when we were little.
I turned out okay.

I let the cats out.
Our two Maine Coons
live in a room
beneath the kitchen. *The basement, Stephanie.*
A finished basement.

Correction: we keep our cats in the basement.

It is frightening
to go either up or down stairs.
They are beginning to sound
human—like us.

iii.

Something in the paint
becomes a hospital;
the leaded cream
embalms
a private bone
black molding
certifies against
the mirrors
and their nook,
hanging here
before the desk,
before the desk, the Askins' window—
no one ever writes without a chair,
I ruined it, I think, watering
the Bonsai, that someone
loved me for.

iv.

If you want to watch TV
you can watch

the news: people say
Southeast Atlanta
police say: a woman

in her home;
a man:
survived: her
husband is:

everyone
on the news is:
off JimmyCarterBoulevard;
sent to Grady

He was:
in the closet
for three days:

she hadn't vacuumed;
he raped her:
I'd've heard:

:what the neighbors said

in a quiet:

brought in,
died.

ELEVATION: NORTH

of the dogs with cords   they spread a net   day and night   your heart goes round it
barking   moves because of piecing   because you hear   the dogs alert—
closer—   nearer now   the chasing   before your pots   can feel
—alert   each closer—   nearer—   nearer dogs   nearer
back   a foot-pace   —evening   they come back   and feel the doors   the lord
that brought me here can count my bones   around it   round it   on its
walls   Awake &   it is not enough   that suddenly
it weighs the heart   that skillful on your lips   I come to ends and walls
I am an object   I have seen a limit   I turn my feet   I hurry

Cataract

the vision of the white lens

how accustomed
her eye has become to it

the collection
of resin
on a slow retina,

precipitous milk
a solid

dandelion
of instant seeds

under the water of all the objects stuck here

fog of furniture,
consuming

a month's worth
of coffee and sugar,

bodies   light in the mouth
of the percolator

orange over rising
water   a darker window   a

white watchcat
spotting her mirrors

removal of the damaged lenses

flat vision

the first sign of health

curves on the table   hard glass

new frames, new
substitute curves
light sent clear
to the kitchen nerve

an immediate winter
a wider room
sutures in

the whites   punctures
near the iris

the pupil can eat all the light you give it

WHEN THE EYE SAW   IT APPEARED

The north produces wind   produces rain

a bird beats into it   around it
        one rises at the sound of birds

How lofty are their eyes   how high
the eyelids lifting

                    there is
                    a lion in
                    your mouth

There is a lion in the street—

          the light they say is near to darkness

the shuttering of door to door

pecked at

                I am full of tossing

full of birds

Pictures of the House Under Construction

Before they broke ground on anything,
they found two beds of copperheads—
at least forty snakes in each.

Every one is quick enough to kill you
but not inclined;
only the babies aren't shy.

Pop once nabbed one
with his walker—see his laugh—
almost better than a drink.

There was a big one
living in the pump room,
bunked below a nest
of unhatched birds.

Locked in, locked out,
it lived in there
until it must have ached from shells;
but it came out

for the party,
and on my birthday,
my father chopped its head off
with a shovel.
You can thank me anytime,
he says.

I found one, swimming in the pool.
Its body shocked and slender
as a drain.
Do you fish it out?
It is electric—
chlorine eats
its scales awake.

Awake, its tail
would snap the net.

This animal is only tail
This animal is tail and snap.

A needle knits me
at both ends.

Educations

For Augusta

A brunette always looks hairier than a blonde.
Valerie Boyd, *The World of Henry Orient*

My mother is culling
our old VHS tapes—
The Flamingo Kid,
The World of Henry Orient,
all those Hitchcocks.

The idea of this
used to break my heart
before our second-to-last VCR broke,
before the film so deteriorated under
Jodie Foster's West Virginia accent,
that now the lambs
will never stop screaming.

I hope you're getting rid
*of that **safety** video, too,*
I whisper to her over the phone
in the dry goods aisle at Walgreens.

She asks,
> *Was is really all that bad—*
> *didn't it teach you about strangers?*

Yes, but—there were other, er, topics...
and there was also singing.

> *Singing?!*

I know there was
something about touching
and something about parts
and a giant dork,
singing about them all,
which was embarrassing because
my sister and I were 9 and 12,
and no one needed to be sung to about that.

And I thought about
the man rinsing out his Speedo
below our balcony
in St. Martin,

and the Swedish girls
we were jealous of
who ran freely
topless at the beach,

and the French girl in my camp cabin
who taught us all
how to fuck our pillows,
and was very enthusiastic,
and I was entranced
to see what she'd need
the pillow for.

Or the junior high assembly
during Christian Emphasis Week,
where we were invited
to promise our bodies to Jesus,
and were admonished by the speaker,
for what he called *heavy petting,*
and I saw us as our older selves,
as enormous, amorous housecats,
pawing each other through furry, quilted oven mitts.

And I wondered what became
of the movies I hoped my mother
didn't know we owned—
Henry and June or *Two Moon Junction*—
the chair scene with Richard Tyson
which I think we'd memorized
the counter number for.

And I thought about
when I did learn those words for parts—
when I was told in school
that I had a v-u-l-v-a,
I wanted to raise my hand and say—
No, I have a vagina
because what was this new and ugly word,
that made all subsequent carpools
in a Volvo furthermore embarrassing?
Vulva is a region,
a smooth, ambiguous place,
like a plastic doll crotch
which legs snap onto.

But I didn't raise my hand,
not even to go to the bathroom,
and then the teacher said

> *Come up and get your drawings, Stephanie—*
> **Stephanie!**

and I, crouched, heel-in-vulva,
stood up, the race to the bathroom already lost,
and sat in the stall until Miss Rudolph came
with her dark eyes, scolding,
handsome as a deer,
and gave me someone else's dry shorts
and a *paper* bag
for my wet things.

Standing now, next to the wholesome bags of prunes,
it seems vulgar to relay the lyrics I suddenly recall,
We all have an anus,
So no matter what you've heard,
Remember that anus,
Is the proper word.
I tell my mother, *It was **bad**. It should be **burned**.* And she tells me,

> *It had to've been better*
> *than the book **my** mother gave to me—*
> *it only talked about FISH!*

.

NATIVE PLANTS AND ANIMALS

For Natalie

Cold— we went with my father
white pine   framing   wet red brick.
You know, you find the veins of it
walky-talkying   back & forth from Earth.

The thought is never fuzzy:
This is what they're doing to the house.

No workers on a Saturday,
just us   my father, working with his camera.
To document the progress
what's yet been done.
The smell of worms unearthing   big bootprints
huffing in and out of mud.

On the temporary staircase   we negotiate
the mess—what used to be the attic   what used to be the roof
the roof removed   the house undressed
the underside   meant for two new rooms.

Understand it will be white:
You can take the lid right off the house.

There are bathtubs in the stairwell wall
pink insulates   pink rolls of foam
a skylight you can never get at
your hand—inspect the air beneath the hole.

To be the driveway   drywall white
the white redbud   the Judas tree
with limbs that bloom against the skin
a branch with cotton in its mouth.

Better to be quizzical   with a set of hands
an architect   with a gauge for depth
a dream we have   of living in the vents
little as The Littles   we even make our tiny beds.

A thumbnail splits the objects far away from you
being smaller.   Pinch them out.

There are animals in the kudzu.
Animals make the news.
The competition: to anatomize this tangle
that yields a skein of woolen skeletons—

an accidental topiary engendered by
the choked out Southern pines
the smothered landscape.

A witness   taking snapshots finds
a sloth of leafy grizzlies   a tower of giraffes
and sends them in to win   what prizes—
being aired on 11-Alive
a t-shirt for your photographs.

There is a memory of elephants,
                    there is a leopard
in the trees   in heat—

        The Florida Police have notified Atlanta
There is a cover crop that forages
where you sleep
            Please look here at the scene here of the accident
All the snakes are pleasing to Police
            Please look here at the position of the occupants

Height in the doorway.

The height of the rise of a stair.

        Police will locate and correct for accident (collision)
        We are pleased to locate
                pleased to look at

Please look here at my mother on the stair—
lotion-sweet   peach terrycloth
as if she just remembered shattering herself.

The mirrors in my stomach flatten.
I never liked the house.

To be the white redbud   a Judas tree
the whitebud branch   dogwooded   urned
tender as a length of skin   and caution-taped
the heart that fills with sieves.

IF SHE IS A WALL   WE BUILD

& if she is a door

a bird of prey   of calling
from far country

with worms to dig   a hook
for catching dinner

> *they kept bringing vessels   &*
> *she kept pouring*

> *I have spoken*
> *and I will bring it*

If she is a wall we build

with scales so near no air can come between them

that carry you from grinding
that carry you from doors

> *can you draw it out*
> *with fishhooks?*

Can you fish its skin?
will traders bargain cord to tongue   lay hands &
think to stir—   this crocodile   your eye lights up on

will you tarry in carrying the sockets?
                    look—

> *the feet are at the door*

around

& one at level

there is an out—

consider

(thinner)

less

the sides

—the locked box

which contains

the ticker

knobs +
ohms +
meters

gas outletted

to the lake.

from upwards

The cabinet-style
which runs

—an antenna

springs

from down in slope

the roof of your mouth

of rooftops

lonelier

blockier

bird-high

a kettle word:

the trees went
    berried

blue lacecaps

thin as acid

better this—

the corner of the house

the short side

pool the scent of   porch   or perch

where they come and check electric

of the earth

but not of houses

Rolling Living Room

Exhaust from an old tailpipe   exhaust in the backseat
from the open car door

from getting in and out   from idling
from someone being helped in   after being waited for

The old two-door with the long front end
sturdy on the outside   solider   collateral

a government-regulated 5 mph bumper
doors as wide as bedsheets   heavy as the kitchen table

A luxury model   pre-Iacocca
a vinyl top   a landau vinyl roof

It squeezes nothing from its passengers
no cut to this carriage   no coupe to this coupe

A tiny silver joystick controls the mirrors
A toggle switch that I can't reach to toggle

The opera window the rear windshield
higher than eye-level and unopenable

A little wind in the pin oaks   a little wind lets in
a brightness   on the scent   of venting

The hum of an air valve   the hum of stale heat
the engine   in the air   condensing

Sharp brown leaves sentinel the driveway
esuriently likes rakes on concrete

—a sound you make at the back of your throat
The drivetrain in the carpet in the hump below my feet

Leather and air from the radiator
the smell of passengers and scalp

Solid on the inside
solid as it shuts things out

ELLEVATION: EAST

It is an old nightmare

clean because its neat and
nothing keeps you there   not

       :windowless   or   :heat

The stairs go down
but still there is no door.

Should I tell about the accident?
It will not keep—

nor you   nor the buttons of a winter coat

it will not keep you smaller

       all the trees went
       : glistening

She might've complained about the smell
but the smell is only near the door

Dryer sheets and gasoline
may soak into the body

and the cement will smooth with oil

For you who say
(to the wood) Wake up!

It will not keep them longer

To the one   a fragrance from
death to death   and to the other   life

The green would haunt you   otherwise
There should not be the door

Similitude

The room that they
have brought us to
is dark   You cannot
see the body
Not because of this
but because of this
you might expect
a service   someone
to officiate
but it's nothing
but waiting
you and the room's
true elephant
handsome as a piece
of furniture   accordingly
appointed   Purposely,
no one is looking
in it   Ask why
it is so dark
why the room
is red   why
the room is always
red   and gracious
as a hotel bar
a red room
like the one
on television   heavy
curtains covering
false windows
a riddle in its sleep
which hastens you
to navigate
an opening   Imagine then
an otherwise clear
night in winter

sharp glass
a quarter-mile from the
Fort George
Island Bridge
the glove compartment
splintering
her chest   And now
so many visitors
cake makeup
a barricade
of tacky wreaths
If navy blue
is dark enough
ask why
you cannot
see the body

ELEVATION: SOUTH

—not sleeping

the edge of the bed

the bed frame   worries itself
in dishes

find: a slipknot
slung by stairs

a stairwell   spun on
as in: needle

a hood-vent
marmalade
ceramic
covers sugar
covers cream

Towels over bowls of rising active yeast

The lord will give
The lord records

Finally
she set the kitchen door ajar

I startled her
right out of her bible—

difficult to see God
with only one good eye

read in
stovelight

                Heavens—

percolate:

      the side-by-side
      makes ice

               Whoever finds its honey

finds a digest: *a garden of*

arthritis

                Heavens—

on her
quilted heart

Wet heat
for the copying
and in copying
the type

her middle finger's
middle   pinks and whites

               Surely God has worn me out

the pencil swells her palm

       *My hands and feet have shriveled
       and I can count my bones*

     It's dark in here,
     Nanny—
          I heard your spoon.

Singers & Dancers alike say:
All my springs are in you

Cleavemark Drive

For Pop

not the live oak—   sand-mount to anthill
you know better   the acorns, yes   —the particularly
silvery asphalt   the *pin*, you say   your house might smell the same

cutting vegetables for chicken I ask you   mid-rib
through breast meat: is it strange to have a craving for liver : and what's a *giblet*
how do you tell the difference between the liver and the heart: so, okay,
like *liverwurst,* what *is* that   —you summon   so exactly
pounds of him to spread on hearty rounds of rye

and standing here over a bowl full of necks   I want to say:
he just handed me a cracker   :but how can I
get its legs off without messing up the skin —growing up in this house again
is like eggshells over eggshells—   you need a pair of scissors
that can cut through bone

Originally from Atlanta, Georgia, Stephanie Ellis Schlaifer is a poet and installation artist in St. Louis, Missouri. She has an MFA from the Iowa Writers' Workshop, and her poems have appeared in *AGNI*, *Denver Quarterly*, *LIT*, *Colorado Review*, *Fence*, and elsewhere. Schlaifer was a semi-finalist for the 2015 Discovery/Boston Review Prize, and she was selected for Best New Poets 2015. She frequently collaborates with other artists, including Jeff Pike on the illustrated chapbook *Strangers with a Lifeboat*, and most recently with Cheryl Wassenaar on an installation at the Fort Gondo Compound for the Arts, based on the poems in *Cleavemark*. Her work can be viewed at criticalbonnet.com.

About the typeface

Garamond Premier (2005) was designed by Robert Slimbach for
Adobe. The design is Slimbach's revisting of the Garamond model after
his Adobe Garamond (1989). It is based on the designs of both Claude
Garamond and Robert Granjon, primarly from sources held by the
Plantin-Moretus museum in Antwerp, Belgium.